First Edition: August 2025

PORTFOLIO RISK MANAGEMENT

THEORETICAL MODELS AND QUANTITATIVE TOOLS TO OPTIMIZE FINANCIAL INVESTMENTS

ABOUT THE AUTHOR

I hold a degree in Economics and have developed extensive expertise in the quantitative management of portfolio risk. Throughout my academic journey, I explored advanced models such as Markowitz optimization, Risk Parity, Value at Risk (VaR), and Expected Shortfall (ES), applying them to real-world portfolio construction. As a retail investor myself, I manage a diversified portfolio that includes both real estate and financial strategies. In this book, I share methodologies and techniques that I have personally tested in practice, directly applying them to portfolio management and investment strategies. My aim is to provide readers with practical, concrete tools to approach financial markets with greater awareness and responsibility.

I present the main theories of risk management with clarity and precision, offering an updated and accessible framework for investors at different levels of experience. Beyond writing, I nurture a strong interest in behavioural finance and remain committed to staying constantly informed about innovations and developments in the financial sector.

Purpose of the Book

1. Provide a solid foundation on the fundamentals of portfolio risk management, distinguishing between systematic and specific risk.
2. Clearly explain the most widely used quantitative risk measures: variance, standard deviation, Beta, and risk matrix.
3. Introduce advanced models such as VaR and Expected Shortfall, including their limitations and practical applications.
4. Present real-world portfolio construction cases: Markowitz model, Risk Parity, and conditional VaR management.

5. Offer an integrated theory-and-practice approach to help readers understand and use quantitative tools consciously in financial investment management.

DISCLAIMER AND DISCLOSURE

Author Disclaimer

The content of this book is provided for informational and educational purposes only and does not constitute personalized financial advice. The analyses, numerical examples, and models are based on theoretical assumptions and historical data. Past results do not guarantee future performance.

The tools described (Markowitz, Risk Parity, VaR, Expected Shortfall) do not take into account the reader's personal profile, financial situation, or specific objectives. This is not an invitation to invest in specific securities, funds, or assets.

Investing involves risks, including potential partial or total loss of capital and market volatility. It is recommended to consult a qualified professional for investment decisions. Neither the author nor the publisher is responsible for any losses the reader may incur from using the information in this book.

Personal Responsibility

The strategies and techniques described in this book require careful evaluation and are to be used at your own risk. The author and the publisher disclaim any liability for direct, indirect, consequential, or incidental losses or damages arising from the use of the information provided. Readers are responsible for independently verifying the content and making informed decisions based on their own judgment and due diligence.

No Professional Advice

The information contained in this book is solely for informational purposes and does not constitute financial, legal, or tax advice. The author is not a registered advisor and does not provide specific recommendations on securities or financial strategies.

No Guarantee of Results

The results described—including past performance and numerical examples—do not guarantee any future outcomes. Actual returns may vary significantly, especially due to unexpected events or market shocks.

No Professional Relationship

Use of this book does not establish a professional relationship between the author and the reader. Any investment decisions are entirely the reader's responsibility.

Acknowledgements

The author acknowledges the contributions of academic courses, industry research, and personal experiences that have enriched the content of this volume. The aim is to offer a comprehensive and practical guide to quantitative portfolio risk management, supported by a wide range of resources and expertise.

Acceptance of Terms

By reading this book, you agree to the terms of this disclaimer. Thank you for your understanding and for joining this journey into finance.

Table of Contents

INTRODUCTION

RISK AND PORTFOLIOS: A NEW QUANTITATIVE PERSPECTIVE

In today's economic-financial context, characterized by increasing globalization and accelerating information flows, portfolio management has become a matter of fundamental importance for both institutional and private investors[1].

Due to the growing complexity of markets and the interdependence among assets of different nature, it has become necessary to resort to new, complex, and scientific methods to make optimal investment decisions. In this environment, quantitative methods applied to portfolio management have emerged as indispensable tools for analysing and managing the mechanisms of risk and return[2].

In the past, investment decisions were primarily based on qualitative analyses, personal intuition, and market expectations; these approaches—once considered valid—are often limited when faced with a vast amount of available data and the volatility of global markets[3]. Portfolio management has been transformed into a more rigorous discipline thanks to the development and use of quantitative methods by analysts, which allow for precise analysis and quantification of fundamental variables such as risk and return. Thanks to algorithms, optimization techniques, and estimation methodologies, investors can make more informed and rational decisions, improving portfolio efficiency and minimizing potential losses.

---

1 Bodie Z., Kane A., & Marcus A. J., *Investments*, McGraw-Hill Education, 2020.

2 Luenberger D. G., *Investment Science*, Oxford University Press., 1998.

3 Markowitz H., *Portfolio Selection*, in *Journal of Finance*, 1952, 7, No. 1.

In this work, the main quantitative approaches to estimating and managing portfolio risk will be explored, with the aim of providing an overview of the methodologies that allow for the construction of more resilient portfolios capable of maximizing the risk-return ratio. Effective risk management does not only imply reducing risk itself, but also understanding and controlling the nature of risk in relation to the investor's objectives[4]. Risk, in fact, is considered an inevitable component of investment activity, but its management allows for improving portfolio profitability by balancing the risk-return trade-off.

The first chapter will introduce the fundamental concepts of portfolio risk management, specifying the difference between systematic risk and specific risk, which are the two main types of risk affecting portfolio performance. Whereas systematic risk is linked to macroeconomic and global factors that cannot be eliminated through diversification, specific risk can be managed and reduced through proper asset selection and diversification. It will then introduce expected utility theory and risk aversion, giving space also to the models for measuring risk aversion.

In the second chapter, which represents the core of the thesis, some risk measures and estimation models are analysed in depth. First, two basic statistical measures are introduced: variance and standard deviation, which quantify the dispersion of returns around the mean and thus estimate the overall volatility of an investment. Next, Beta is examined—a measure that evaluates an asset's sensitivity to market fluctuations; Beta is also an indispensable parameter of the Capital Asset Pricing Model (CAPM), which allows for estimating expected return as a function of risk. This section also addresses the traditional risk matrix, a useful tool for classifying and comparing types of risk and evaluating overall portfolio exposure.

Subsequently, the Value at Risk (VaR) is examined—a measure that calculates the expected maximum loss over a given time interval at a specified confidence level. Alternative VaR calculation methods (parametric, historical, and Monte Carlo) are considered, as well as the Expected Shortfall (ES), a more robust risk measure that estimates potential losses in extreme scenarios.

---

[4] Jorion P., *Value at Risk: The New Benchmark for Managing Financial Risk*, McGraw-Hill, 2007.

In the third chapter, the Markowitz model and the main portfolio risk management techniques are analysed using two principal approaches: the Risk Parity method and the VaR-based method. The first model analysed is based on the works of Markowitz and is discussed both theoretically and practically, including an analysis of how to construct an optimal portfolio. Later, the Risk Parity method—aimed at balancing risk across assets to minimize concentration on a single asset class—and the VaR method, intended to keep overall risk within acceptable thresholds, are presented.

The main purpose of this thesis is to investigate and critically and systematically analyse the quantitative methods applied to portfolio management, with particular attention to risk management.

Today, quantitative models—thanks to advances in computing technologies and increased data availability—have become an essential resource for fund managers, institutional investors, and financial advisors; however, it must be emphasized that these instruments are not without limitations and issues, which will be discussed throughout the thesis. In particular, it will be highlighted how excessive reliance on quantitative models can lead to overestimating predictive capacity and underestimating rare and unforeseen events, known as "black swans."

Precisely to avoid underestimating rare events, it is essential to recognize the limits of mathematical models and know how to integrate them with a broader and more flexible market perspective.

CHAPTER 1

THE FUNDAMENTALS OF PORTFOLIO RISK MANAGEMENT

One of the principal challenges that fund managers and investors face in their work is managing portfolio risk. Some essential steps to ensure investment goals are reached efficiently include understanding risk, measuring it accurately, and adopting strategies to mitigate it[5]. This chapter explores the concept of risk with particular attention to its systematic and specific nature. It also introduces expected utility theory and risk aversion, providing an explanation of models that measure risk aversion[6].

1.1. Introduction to risk management

In the financial field, risk is defined as the probability that the actual results of an investment differ from the expected ones. The main aspects that can have a negative impact on a portfolio's performance can be identified in various economic, political, and market-specific factors. The primary objective of risk management is to identify, measure, and, if possible, mitigate these factors.

Risk management is closely linked to the decision regarding the level of risk that the investor is willing to tolerate in order to achieve a certain return; in this sense, it is not about eliminating risk, but about managing it consciously according to the investor's objectives. In this approach, the risk-return concept is central because

[5] Bodie Z., Kane A., Marcus A. J., *Investments.*, cit., p. 3.

[6] Pratt J. W., *Risk Aversion in the Small and in the Large*, in *Econometrica*, 1964, 32 No. 1-2.

higher risk generally entails a higher potential return, but also a greater probability of incurring losses.

Therefore, in this context, to correctly evaluate the risk of a portfolio and adopt the necessary hedging and optimization strategies, the application of quantitative tools is essential.

1.2. Systematic risk and specific risk

The distinction between systematic risk (or market risk) and specific risk (or idiosyncratic risk) is one of the first fundamental distinctions to understand in risk management. By analysing the two types of risk individually, it can be stated that:

- Systematic risk is a risk that concerns the entire market or an entire economic sector and cannot be eliminated through diversification. It is caused by macroeconomic factors such as inflation, interest rates, global economic crises, monetary policies, and trend changes at the national or international level. Since it affects all assets uniformly, it is also called "market risk." The main characteristics of systematic risk are the lack of diversification, the broad impact, and positive correlation.

  To effectively manage systematic risk, strategies are used that aim to reduce exposure to it, such as the use of derivative instruments, dynamic asset allocation management, and hedging through investments in assets less correlated with the economic cycle, such as so-called safe-haven assets[7].
- Specific risk, also known as idiosyncratic risk or unsystematic risk, is linked to factors exclusive to a single company or a specific sector. Analysing this type of risk, in particular, it can be stated that it derives, for example, from changes in the demand for a certain product or sector, from managerial choices of a single company, or from unique events affecting a single security. Specific risk, unlike systematic risk, can be reduced through portfolio diversification[8], that is, by investing in a wide range of uncorrelated

---

[7] Hull J. C., *Risk Management and Financial Institutions*, Wiley, 2015.

[8] Markowitz H., *Portfolio Selection*, in *The Journal of Finance*, p. 3.

securities. Diversification is considered effective when it includes diversification by sector, geographical area, and asset class.

In addition to systematic risk and specific risk, there is another type of risk: total risk. The total risk of a portfolio is the result of the combination of systematic risk and specific risk. The percentage presence of the two risks differs in every portfolio, and in a well-diversified portfolio, specific risk tends to be almost completely reduced, leaving systematic risk as the predominant source of uncertainty; on the other hand, in a poorly diversified portfolio, specific risk may represent a significant portion of the total risk. From a mathematical point of view, the total risk of a portfolio can be represented as the sum of the components of systematic risk and specific risk.

1.3. Utility theory and risk aversion

The theory of utility is one of the cornerstones of economics and aims to better understand how decisions are made under conditions of uncertainty. In general, risk-averse people prefer investments with lower risk even if this means lower returns, unlike risk-seeking individuals, for whom return is the most important variable, even if associated with significantly higher risks.

This theory[9] was developed by two mathematical economists (John von Neumann and Oskar Morgenstern) at the end of the Second World War, and its main goal was to identify the mechanisms by which people make decisions under uncertainty, based on maximizing their expected utility—that is, the level of well-being that a certain economic outcome produces for them.

Mathematically, expected utility is calculated by summing the product of the probability of each possible outcome by the utility of the outcome itself:

$$U(x) = \sum_{i} p_i \, u(x_i) \tag{1}$$

where:

- $U(x)$ is the expected utility of the investor,
- p_i represents the probability of each possible outcome,

[9] Von Neumann J., Morgenstern O., *Theory of Games and Economic Behavior,* 1944, Princeton University Press.

- $u(x_i)$ is the utility associated with the outcome x_i.

Therefore, individuals choose the alternative that provides the highest level of expected utility, even if this does not always coincide with maximizing the expected value in purely monetary terms.

One of the fundamental aspects of utility theory is the distinction between different types of individuals: risk-averse, risk-neutral, and risk-seeking. The attitude a person has toward risk directly affects investment decisions and the type of portfolio chosen. By analysing the three types of investors specifically, we can state that:

- Risk-averse investors are the majority, meaning that an investor prefers to avoid uncertainty and negative fluctuations in their investments. The utility function of a risk-averse investor is concave with respect to wealth, implying that the increase in utility generated by an additional unit of wealth is diminishing. This type of investor prefers portfolios that, for the same expected return, involve the lowest risk[10].
- Risk-neutral investors are those who evaluate investment decisions exclusively on the basis of expected return, without considering risk. In this case, utility is a linear function of wealth, and these individuals neither penalize nor reward more or less risky portfolios.
- Risk-seeking investors are individuals who prefer more volatile portfolios, provided that the expected return is the same as less risky alternatives. In this case, the utility function is convex with respect to wealth, and the possibility of achieving high gains justifies the risk.

1.3.1. Utility curve and risk aversion

The utility curve represents the relationship between risk and utility and is graphically depicted on a Cartesian plane, where the horizontal axis shows the risk of an investment, generally identified by a measure of volatility such as variance or standard

[10] Pratt J. W., *Risk Aversion in the Small and in the Large*, in *Econometrica*, p. 6.

deviation (discussed in detail in sections 2.1 and 2.1.1), and the vertical axis shows the level of utility.

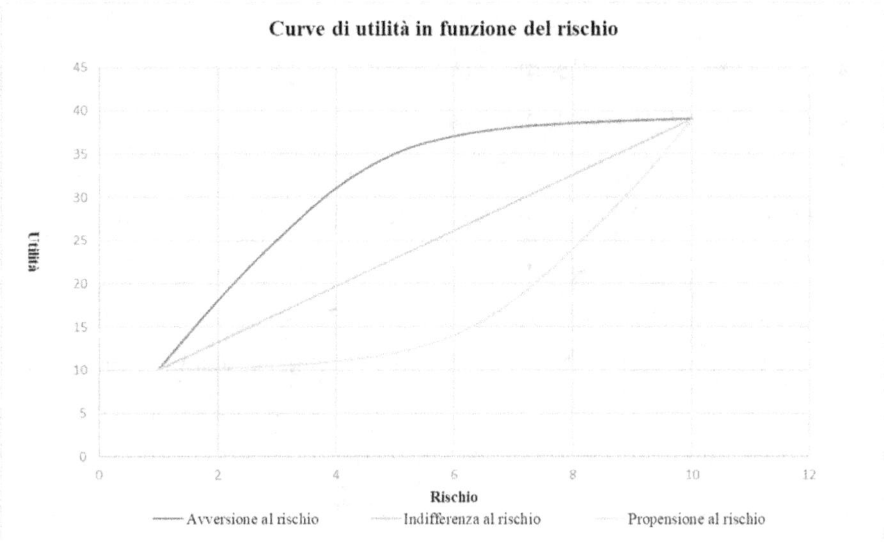

Figure 1 – Utility curves as a function of risk[11]

This representation also makes it possible to understand the extent to which a person is willing to take on progressively increasing risks in exchange for increases in returns, and to determine whether we are dealing with a risk-averse or risk-seeking person. In particular, the concave shape of the function is typical of risk-averse individuals (see Fig. 1 Utility curves as a function of risk), meaning that after a certain level of risk, any further increase is not considered by the investor to be compensated by the corresponding increase in the utility function, which flattens out after a certain level of risk.

The risk aversion of an investor influences the percentage allocation of high- and low-risk assets. Risk-averse investors tend to prefer a greater allocation to bonds, government securities, or assets with reduced volatility, while reserving a smaller share for equity investments.

Conversely, less risk-averse investors may focus on equities and more aggressive portfolios, with greater exposure to potentially wider fluctuations.

[11] Author's own elaboration

The utility curve of a risk-neutral investor (see Fig. 1 Utility curves as a function of risk), on the other hand, is a straight line, as it shows a linear relationship between risk and utility, meaning that a risk-neutral investor is indifferent to the level of risk and evaluates utility proportionally to the expected return, without having a preference for either seeking or avoiding risk.

By contrast, the utility curve of a risk-seeking person is convex (see Fig. 1 Utility curves as a function of risk), with incremental values of risk associated with higher returns and an increasingly greater marginal utility.

The saver is therefore inclined to accept investments with progressively increasing risks, because in that range of risk, their marginal utility grows more than proportionally.

The utility theory thus helps to define the optimal portfolio for each investor, based on their specific risk tolerance. The optimal portfolio for a rational investor is not only the one that maximizes returns, but the one that, for a given level of risk, provides the highest utility.

1.3.2. Models for measuring risk aversion

The ability to measure and quantify risk aversion is essential to define investment strategies consistent with investors' preferences; indeed, only in this way can a balance be found between expected return and variability of outcomes. To correctly quantify and interpret risk aversion, several models have been developed over the years, each with its own characteristics and specific objectives. One of the first methods to measure risk aversion was introduced by Arrow and Pratt, through the Absolute Risk Aversion index (ARA) and the Relative Risk Aversion index (RRA). Both provide a measure of how risk-averse an individual is, using the utility function as a reference: Specifically, the Absolute Risk Aversion (ARA) index is measured as:

$$ARA = -\frac{u''(W)}{u'(W)} \tag{2}$$

where:

- $u(W)$ is the utility function of wealth W,

- $u'(W)$ is the first derivative of the utility function with respect to wealth, i.e., the marginal utility of wealth. It indicates how much utility changes for a marginal increase in wealth,
- $u''(W)$ is the second derivative of the utility function with respect to wealth, representing the curvature of the utility function. This measures the change in marginal utility as wealth varies and provides information on risk aversion.

This formula expresses how much the investor is willing to give up in terms of return for a marginal reduction in risk. A high ARA indicates that the investor is highly risk-averse, while a low ARA suggests a greater willingness to take risks. The utility function is defined based on the risk aversion coefficient as:

- Constant Absolute Risk Aversion (CARA)[12], or utility function with constant absolute risk aversion if ARA is constant with respect to W,
- Decreasing Absolute Risk Aversion (DARA), or utility function with decreasing absolute risk aversion if ARA decreases as W increases,
- Increasing Absolute Risk Aversion (IARA), or utility function with increasing absolute risk aversion if ARA increases as W increases.

Instead, the Relative Risk Aversion (RRA) index is calculated as:

$$RRA = -W \cdot \frac{u''(W)}{u'(W)} \tag{3}$$

where:

- W is the investor's wealth,
- $u(W)$ is the utility function, which describes the degree of satisfaction or utility the investor derives from their wealth,
- $u'(W)$ represents the first derivative of the utility function with respect to wealth, i.e., the marginal utility of wealth. It indicates how utility changes with a marginal increase in wealth,
- $u''(W)$ represents the second derivative of the utility function with respect to wealth, i.e., the change in marginal utility of wealth. It helps to understand

---

[12] Linciano N., Soccorso P., *La rilevazione della tolleranza al rischio degli investitori attraverso il questionario*, CONSOB, July 2012.

how marginal utility changes as wealth varies and thus indicates the level of risk aversion.

The Relative Risk Aversion index therefore measures how much an investor is willing to risk not only in relation to their utility curve but also according to their available wealth. This indicator thus helps explain why investors with the same level of risk aversion (i.e., with the same utility curve) behave differently depending on how much money they have. Usually, individuals show increasing relative risk aversion, meaning they tend to be willing to risk a larger proportion of their wealth as their wealth increases.

From a practical standpoint, these risk aversion measurement models are directly applied in portfolio construction to determine the optimal combination between return and risk. For example, an investor with a high ARA index will tend to build portfolios composed mainly of low-risk assets, while an investor with a low ARA might prefer a portfolio more oriented towards high-yield and thus higher variability assets. Measuring risk aversion is also essential for dynamic portfolio allocation; indeed, investors can modify their allocation strategies based on changes in their risk tolerance and market variability.

CHAPTER 2

THE METHODS AND MODELS FOR RISK ESTIMATION

In the process of constructing and analysing an investment portfolio, risk management is a fundamental element. To effectively estimate and control a portfolio's risk exposure, a quantitative approach must be employed through the use of mathematical models and statistical methods. The ability to measure risk accurately is essential in portfolio management, as it allows investors to adopt more effective strategies for diversification, hedging, and capital allocation. It should also be noted that the ability to estimate potential losses helps ensure the long-term sustainability of the portfolio, thus limiting the risk of default or excessive losses in the event of market shocks.

In this second section of the work, the main models and methods used to measure risk in portfolio management will be introduced and analysed, with particular emphasis on metrics such as variance and standard deviation, Beta, the traditional risk matrix, and indicators such as Value at Risk (VaR) and Expected Shortfall (ES). All of the aforementioned tools are essential, as each allows the detection and provision of different perspectives on investment volatility and risk.

2.1. Variance

The first metric I will analyse is variance, a measure used to estimate risk, which indicates the dispersion of an asset's or portfolio's returns relative to their mean. Variance is one of the fundamental measures of risk in finance because it reflects the volatility of returns, that is, their tendency to fluctuate over time. Operationally, the higher the variance, the more the returns of the asset or portfolio deviate from their mean, indicating a higher level of risk. Often, to assess the risk of an investment, variance is used together with the standard deviation, which corresponds to the square root of the variance itself.

One of the characteristics that makes variance a particularly valued measure is that it allows the comparison of the risk of different assets and portfolios. This feature is important because investors are generally risk-averse and prefer portfolios with lower risk. Despite its usefulness, variance does not distinguish between positive and negative deviations of returns (since all deviations from the mean are squared), but it still provides the investor with an indication of the overall level of uncertainty associated with an investment.

2.1.1. Definition and calculation of variance and standard deviation

From a mathematical perspective, variance (σ^2) is defined as the average of the squares of the deviations of individual values from their mean. Operationally, it is calculated by summing the squares of the deviations of each individual value (in this case, return) from the mean and then dividing the result by the total number of observations. One of the aspects that makes variance a valuable parameter is that by squaring the deviations, negative differences are eliminated, so that positive and negative fluctuations relative to the mean carry the same weight. This allows for a precise measure of the overall dispersion of the data.

In finance, the variance of an asset's or portfolio's returns reflects the probability that the actual return will differ from the expected return, implying the presence of associated risk.

The general formula for variance for a single asset is:

$$\sigma^2 = \frac{1}{N}\sum_{i=1}^{N}(R_i - \mu)^2 \tag{4}$$

Where:

- σ^2 represents the variance of the asset,
- R_i is the return of the asset in period i,
- μ is the mean return of the asset,
- N is the total number of observations.

Specifically, this formula shows how much returns R_i deviate from their mean (μ), providing an estimate of the overall volatility of the asset.

For a portfolio composed of multiple assets, the calculation of variance becomes more complex because it must consider not only the variance of each asset but also the correlation among the assets. Correlation measures the degree to which the returns of two assets move in relation to each other, significantly affecting portfolio risk. Two assets perfectly positively correlated increase overall risk, whereas two negatively correlated assets can help reduce total portfolio risk through diversification.

The variance of a portfolio with multiple assets is given by:

$$\sigma_p^2 = \sum_{i=1}^{n}\sum_{j=1}^{n} w_i\, w_j \text{Cov}(R_i, R_j) \tag{5}$$

Where:

- σ_p^2 is the portfolio variance,
- w_i and w_j are the weights of assets i and j in the portfolio,
- $\text{Cov}(R_i, R_j)$ is the covariance between returns of assets i and j,
- n is the number of assets in the portfolio.

This formula shows that the total risk of a portfolio depends not only on the variance of individual assets but also on their covariance. Covariance measures the extent to which the returns of two assets move together. Positive covariance means that returns tend to move in the same direction; negative covariance means they tend to move in opposite directions. Portfolio diversification aims to combine assets with low or negative covariance to reduce overall risk.

Despite being widely used, variance[13] has some limitations. First, as noted earlier, it does not distinguish between positive and negative variations, which can be an issue for investors particularly concerned about losses. A second limitation is its assumption that returns are normally distributed, which often does not reflect real financial markets that can show asymmetrical distributions and extreme events.

Another limitation is that variance cannot separate systematic and unsystematic risk. As previously mentioned, diversification can reduce unsystematic risk, but variance alone cannot distinguish the two components. To overcome these limitations, variance in finance should always be used alongside other metrics, such as Value at Risk (VaR) and Expected Shortfall (ES), to provide a comprehensive view of investment risk.

Closely related to variance is standard deviation, a statistical measure representing the dispersion of data around its mean, also known as the root mean square deviation. Standard deviation is widely applied in data management, scientific, and financial contexts. In finance, it is used to assess the volatility of a security or portfolio, indicating how much actual returns deviate from expected average returns. This parameter is essential for evaluating investment risk, as higher volatility is considered synonymous with higher risk.

Standard deviation[14] is calculated from variance, which measures the average dispersion of returns from their mean. By taking the positive square root of variance, standard deviation scales the measure to the same units as the returns.

The mathematical formula for standard deviation σ for a series of returns $R_1, R_2, \ldots, R_N$ is:

$$\sigma = \sqrt{\frac{1}{N}\sum_{i=1}^{N}(R_i - \mu)^2} \tag{6}$$

Where:

- N is the number of observations (or periods),

---

[13] Kelly Price, Barbara Price, Timothy J. Nantell, *Variance and Lower Partial Moment Measures of Systematic Risk: Some Analytical and Empirical Results* in *Journal of Finance*, 1982 No. 3.

[14] Michael B. Miller, *Quantitative Financial Risk Management*, Wiley, 2019.

- R_i is the observed return in period i,
- μ is the mean return over N periods.

This formula can be applied to individual securities or portfolios and serves as a starting point for risk management. Volatility and risk are closely linked: a more volatile asset has more unpredictable returns, implying higher risk. A high standard deviation indicates that an investment's returns are widely dispersed relative to the mean, reflecting greater risk, whereas a low standard deviation suggests lower variability and thus lower risk.

Since standard deviation is the square root of variance, it shares similar applications and limitations:

- Equal treatment of deviations: Both positive and negative deviations from the mean are treated equally.
- Assumption of normal distribution: Standard deviation assumes returns are normally distributed, which is often not true in real financial markets that exhibit fatter tails. Extreme events, such as financial crises, have a larger impact than a normal distribution predicts.
- Underestimation of extreme risks: Standard deviation tends to underestimate tail risk, which occurs less frequently but has significant impact. To address this, advanced metrics such as VaR or ES are used alongside standard deviation.
- Historical measure: Standard deviation is based on historical data, which can limit its predictive usefulness. Future volatility may differ from past levels due to changes in markets, economic policies, or other macro factors. In such cases, ARCH models can be adopted to forecast conditional variance.

2.1.2. Alternative variance estimation methods

In many real-world contexts, using classical variance alone as a measure of the dispersion of returns of a portfolio or an asset is insufficient to capture the complexity of financial markets. For this reason, advanced methods for calculating variance have been developed, capable of providing a more accurate, forward-looking, and detailed view of risk. These methods focus on the dynamic nature of variance over time, asset correlations, and heteroscedasticity (non-constant variance over time).

One of the most widely used models to capture the temporal variability of variance is the ARCH (Autoregressive Conditional Heteroskedasticity) model and its extension, GARCH (Generalized Autoregressive Conditional Heteroskedasticity)[15]. Another model used to estimate variance is the EWMA (Exponentially Weighted Moving Average). These models assume that the variance of an asset is not constant over time but depends on past residual terms. This is particularly useful in contexts where volatility tends to change significantly, such as during financial crises or periods of high market instability.

The ARCH model is a precursor to the GARCH model and is used to estimate conditional variance. Unlike classical variance, which assumes constancy over time, the ARCH model allows variance to change from period to period based on past observations[16].

The general form of an ARCH(q) model is:

$$\sigma_t^2 = \alpha_0 + \sum_{i=1}^{q} \alpha_i \, \epsilon_{t-i}^2 \tag{7}$$

Where:

- σ_t^2 is the conditional variance at time t,
- ϵ_{t-i} is the past forecast error (i.e., the difference between expected and actual return),
- α_0 and α_i are parameters to estimate,
- q is the number of past errors considered.

This model is particularly useful in the presence of heteroscedasticity, that is, when the variance of a time series is not constant. The ARCH model effectively identifies volatility dynamics in a time series but is limited because it does not consider the temporal dependence of variance itself, which is included in the GARCH model.

[15] Bollerslev T., *Generalized Autoregressive Conditional Heteroskedasticity* in *Journal of Econometrics*, 1986, No. 31.
[16] Tsay R. S., *Analysis of Financial Time Series* (3rd ed.), Wiley-Interscience 2010.

Building on the ARCH model, one of the most advanced methods for variance calculation was developed: the GARCH model. It captures the dynamics of volatility over time. While classical variance assumes constant return volatility, the GARCH model recognizes that volatility often fluctuates in many markets. This model is particularly useful for analysing periods of financial turbulence or economic crises, when volatility rises sharply.

The GARCH model assumes that an asset's return variance can also be influenced by past volatility. Practically, the model incorporates an autoregressive component (dependence of variance on past values) and a heteroscedastic component (dependence of variance on past forecast errors).

The general form of a GARCH (p, q) model is:

$$\sigma_t^2 = \alpha_0 + \sum_{i=1}^{q} \alpha_i \, \epsilon_{t-i}^2 + \sum_{j=1}^{p} \beta_j \, \sigma_{t-j}^2 \tag{8}$$

Where:

- σ_t^2 is the conditional variance at time t,
- ϵ_{t-i} represents the forecast error at time $t - i$,
- α_0, α_i and β_j are parameters to estimate,
- q is the number of forecast error terms included,
- p is the number of past conditional variance terms considered.

The GARCH model is effective in capturing the volatility clustering effect, i.e., the tendency of high-volatility periods to be followed by other high-volatility periods and vice versa.

Another important model for dynamic variance calculation is the EWMA[17] model. This model assumes that past returns have a decreasing weight over time in determining current variance; consequently, it assigns an exponentially decreasing weight to past returns, giving more emphasis to recent events.

The EWMA model formula is:

$$\sigma_t^2 = \lambda \sigma_{t-1}^2 + (1 - \lambda) R_{t-1}^2 \tag{9}$$

Where:

---

[17] J.P. Morgan, *RiskMetrics—Technical Document*. J.P. Morgan/Reuters, 1996.

- σ_t^2 is the estimated variance at time t,
- σ_{t-1}^2 is the estimated variance at the previous time $t-1$,
- R_{t-1}^2 is the squared return observed at time $t-1$,
- λ is a smoothing parameter that assigns greater weight to recent returns and less to older returns.

The λ parameter typically ranges between 0.94 and 0.97 and determines the speed at which past returns lose importance in variance calculation. For example, with λ = 0.94, older returns are rapidly discounted compared to more recent ones. This method is useful when volatility changes frequently, as in highly dynamic markets.

There is also another approach for estimating variance: the Monte Carlo simulation method, a more sophisticated approach for estimating variance and risk. It simulates thousands of possible scenarios for future returns of an asset or portfolio to obtain an empirical distribution of variance.

The intrinsic feature of this model is its ability to incorporate random and nonlinear variables that often influence markets, and it is not constrained by the assumption of normal distribution typical of other methods. Variance via the Monte Carlo method is calculated based on randomly generated future scenarios, with inputs derived from historical data or specific hypotheses. The flexibility of this approach is one of its main advantages, as it can adapt to any distribution or market behavior model. A critical aspect of this model is its high computational demand and the complexity of practical implementation.

2.2. Beta and notes on CAPM

The Beta coefficient (β)[18] expresses the relationship between the return of a security or of a portfolio R_i and the return of the reference market R_m, quantified as the ratio between the covariance of the returns of the security and the market and the variance of the market returns:

$$\beta = \frac{\text{Cov}(R_i, R_m)}{\text{Var}(R_m)} \tag{10}$$

[18] Kenton W., *What Beta Means for Investors* in *Investopedia*, 2024.

Where:

- Cov(R_i, R_m) is the covariance between the returns of the security i and the market,
- Var(R_m) is the variance of the market returns.

The ratio between the dynamic covariance of an asset and the market and the variance of the latter provides a measure of the reactivity of the security to market fluctuations.

A practical way to estimate Beta is through a linear regression of the security's return on the market returns, which is expressed through the following formula:

$$R_i = \alpha + \beta R_m + \epsilon \tag{11}$$

Where:

- R_i is the return of the i-th security,
- R_m is the market return,
- α is the intercept of the regression line,
- β is the regression coefficient (that is, the Beta of the security),
- ϵ is the residual term.

The value of β is obtained by minimizing the sum of the squares of the differences between the observed values and theoretical values (minimization of squared errors), a process that can be executed using statistical software or by manually calculating the covariance and variance of the returns of the security and the market.

The Beta coefficient represents a fundamental tool for quantifying the systematic risk of a security or a portfolio relative to the market. In the context of portfolio risk management, Beta provides an indication of the sensitivity of an asset's return with respect to the movements of a market index, such as, for example, a stock index. This metric is also used to understand and manage the risk associated with general market movements.

In the process of evaluating the risk of an investment, Beta is one of the most important indicators thanks to its characteristics. Analysing specifically the values that the Beta coefficient can assume, we can identify some main characteristics:

- β > 1: The presence of a Beta greater than 1 indicates that the security is more sensitive to market movements. For example, a Beta of 1.5 implies that the security will tend to move 50% more than the market changes. If the market rises by 10%, the security with Beta 1.5 will increase by 15%; obviously, this situation corresponds to higher losses in the case of a market decline. From this point of view, we can classify it as an aggressive security.
- β = 1: If the Beta of a security is equal to 1, it means that the security moves in line with the market. In other words, if the market increases by 5%, the security will also increase by 5%, and vice versa in the case of a decline. From this point of view, we can classify it as an indexed security.
- β < 1: A Beta less than 1 indicates that the security is less volatile than the market. For example, a Beta of 0.7 implies that if the market rises by 10%, the security will move only by 7%. This type of asset tends to be less risky, but also offers lower returns. From this point of view, we can classify it as a defensive security.
- β < 0: In rare cases, some securities can have a negative Beta, which means that they tend to move in the opposite direction relative to the market. For example, assets such as gold or certain safe-haven assets may have a negative Beta, since they often increase in value when financial markets are in crisis. From this point of view, we can classify it as a counter-cyclical asset.

One of the main applications of the Beta coefficient is the Capital Asset Pricing Model (CAPM); in fact, Beta is an essential component of the CAPM[19].

The Capital Asset Pricing Model (CAPM) is one of the most widely used models in finance to determine the expected return of an investment, based on its level of systematic risk relative to the market. This tool was developed in the 1960s by William Sharpe and John Lintner and allows calculating the required return for a security or a portfolio as a function of non-diversifiable risk, represented by Beta. The main formula of the CAPM is:

---

[19] Sharpe W. F., *Capital Asset Prices: A Theory of Market Equilibrium under Conditions of Risk*, in *Journal of Finance*, 1964, 19 No. 3.

$$E(R_i) = R_f + \beta_i \times \left(E(R_m) - R_f\right) \tag{12}$$

Where:

- $E(R_i)$ is the expected return of the i-th security,
- R_f is the risk-free rate (such as a government bond yield),
- β_i is the sensitivity of the security relative to market movements (the Beta of the i-th security),
- $E(R_m)$ is the expected market return,
- $E(R_m) - R_f$ represents the market risk premium.

One of the assumptions of CAPM is that investors are risk-averse and therefore are willing to invest in securities with higher systematic risk only if these offer a higher expected return. The model distinguishes systematic risk, which cannot be eliminated through diversification, from specific risk, which can instead be reduced by diversifying the portfolio.

The CAPM[20] has become a fundamental tool for the valuation of securities, in estimating the cost of capital for companies, and in constructing optimal portfolios due to its simplicity and clarity; at the same time, however, it also has limitations, such as the assumption that Beta is constant over time and that all investors share the same market expectations.

Beta, despite its validity as a risk measure and the numerous models that use it, presents some limitations:

- Dependence on historical data: The Beta coefficient is calculated using historical return data, which implies that it is a retrospective measure. Consequently, Beta may not accurately represent the future sensitivity of a security to market variations. If market conditions change, historical Betas become less relevant.
- Does not capture specific risk: Beta measures exclusively systematic risk, that is, the risk related to general market movements, but does not consider specific or idiosyncratic risk, which is linked to particular factors of a single

---

[20] Fama E. F., French K. R., (2004) *The Capital Asset Pricing Model: Theory and Evidence*, in *Journal of Economic Perspectives*, 2004, 18 No. 3.

security or company. This implies that two securities with the same Beta may have very different risk levels if we consider specific risk.

- Dependence on the reference index: Beta is calculated relative to a market index, and its interpretation depends on the choice of such an index. If a security is compared with an inappropriate index, Beta may be misleading. This can be particularly problematic for global portfolios or those including securities from uncorrelated markets.
- Variation of Beta over time: The Beta of a security is not static and can vary over time, especially due to changes in the company structure, economic policies, or market conditions.
- Non-linear effects: Beta assumes a linear relationship between the security returns and the market returns, but in reality, this relationship may not be perfectly linear, especially in extremely volatile markets or during crisis periods. In these cases, Beta may underestimate or overestimate the actual risk associated with a security.

2.3. Traditional risk matrix

The traditional risk matrix is an analytical tool used in the field of finance to evaluate and classify the risk associated with different assets within a portfolio. In practical terms, this matrix allows representing in a schematic way the total risk of a portfolio which, as mentioned previously, can be broken down into systematic risk (market risk) and specific risk (idiosyncratic risk), and aims to provide an overall picture that enables investors to make decisions based on an objective quantification of risk.

The function of the matrix, to compare different investments both in terms of risk and return, allows providing the investor with an evaluation of performance, risk control, and indications on portfolio diversification.

The two main metrics on which the matrix is based are standard deviation and the Beta coefficient, two fundamental measures to consider systematic risk and the volatility of an asset relative to the entire market.

The traditional risk matrix, although a fundamental tool, presents some critical issues:

- Assumption of normal distribution: The traditional matrix is based on measures, such as standard deviation, which assume a normal distribution of returns. Consequently, in the event of extreme market movements, the traditional matrix would not be able to capture them.
- Assumption of stationarity: Metrics such as Beta and standard deviation rely on historical data, considering the past behaviour of an asset as a good indicator for the future. Very often, in rapidly changing financial markets, these measures may prove insufficient.
- Ability to capture extreme risks: The traditional risk matrix does not consider tail risks, i.e., rare events but with significant impacts, such as financial crises. To address this type of risk, more advanced methods have been developed, such as Value at Risk (VaR) and Expected Shortfall (ES).

2.4. Value at Risk (VaR)

Value at Risk (VaR)[21] is one of the most widely used risk measures in the financial world to quantify the risk of loss associated with an investment portfolio. It is a fundamental tool for portfolio managers, financial institutions, and investors, as it makes it possible to estimate, with a certain degree of confidence, the maximum loss a portfolio may incur within a given time horizon. In fact, VaR provides a clear and direct answer to the question: "What is the maximum loss a portfolio may suffer with a given probability (for example 95% or 99%) within a specified time interval?" The concept of VaR became a global standard in risk management starting in the 1990s, and particularly from 1994 when J.P. Morgan published its VaR calculation model called RiskMetrics[22], making the software and data freely available; from that moment, all major financial institutions and regulatory authorities began to adopt it as a measure to assess portfolio risk, determine capital requirements, control market risk, and evaluate performance.

[21] Dowd K., *Measuring Market Risk*, Wiley, 2002.
[22] J.P. Morgan, *RiskMetrics—Technical Document*, p. 20.

The simplicity and intuitiveness of VaR are two aspects that make this measure appealing; a manager can, in fact, quickly understand how much risk is associated with a portfolio and make informed decisions to mitigate it. The VaR metric specifically analyses the lower tail of the return distribution and, more precisely, quantifies the risk associated with extreme events that occur with a low, yet not negligible, probability.

2.4.1. Definition and calculation of VaR

As already introduced in paragraph (2.4), Value at Risk (VaR) is a statistical measure used to estimate the maximum potential loss of a financial portfolio within a given time horizon and with a certain confidence level.

In formal terms, the VaR with a confidence level α is defined as the maximum potential loss that a portfolio can incur within a certain time horizon t, with a probability of $1-\alpha$. This means that there is a probability α that losses will exceed the value estimated by the VaR. For example, if the VaR is calculated at a 95% confidence level for one day, there is a 5% probability that the actual loss will exceed the VaR in a single trading day.

Mathematically, the VaR can be expressed as:

$$P(\text{Loss} > \text{VaR}) = 1 - \alpha \tag{13}$$

Where:

- α is the confidence level (e.g., 95% or 99%),
- $P(\text{Loss} > \text{VaR})$ is the probability that the loss is greater than the VaR.

VaR can be calculated in different ways, and the main ones are:

- the Parametric method (variance-covariance),
- the Historical method,
- the Monte Carlo Simulation method.

All these methods have different advantages and disadvantages, which will be described and analysed in this chapter.

The Parametric method, also known as the variance-covariance method, is based on the assumption that the returns of financial assets are normally distributed, i.e., they follow a Gaussian distribution. This method requires the use of the mean and the standard deviation of historical returns to estimate the maximum expected loss.

The parametric VaR can be calculated using the following formula:

$$VaR = \mu + z_\alpha \cdot \sigma \tag{14}$$

Where:

- μ is the expected return of the portfolio,
- z_α is the critical value of the normal distribution corresponding to the confidence level α,
- σ is the standard deviation of returns, which measures the portfolio's volatility.

This approach is widely used due to its simplicity of implementation and the ease with which it can be applied to large portfolios, but it has a limitation linked to the assumption of a normal distribution of returns, which may underestimate risk when markets experience extreme movements or non-normal distributions (e.g., fat tails).

The Historical method, on the other hand, is a non-parametric approach that does not require the assumption of a normal distribution of returns, but instead relies on the analysis of historical data to estimate VaR. In this method, past returns of a portfolio or a single asset are collected and arranged in ascending order. The VaR is then determined by selecting the loss corresponding to the chosen percentile for the confidence level.

For example, if one wishes to calculate the VaR at 95%, the loss corresponding to the 5th percentile of historical returns will be selected.

The main advantages of this method are that it directly reflects the volatility observed in the past and does not require assumptions about the distribution of returns, while its main drawback is linked to the use of past data, which may not be representative of future risks, especially under extraordinary market conditions.

Another approach to calculating VaR is the Monte Carlo simulation method, which is based on simulating a large number of possible market scenarios. This model uses probabilistic assumptions to simulate a series of possible future scenarios for asset prices or returns. Subsequently, the loss associated with each scenario is calculated, and the VaR is determined by identifying the loss level corresponding to the desired percentile.

The Monte Carlo method is used for complex portfolios, which contain derivative instruments or are exposed to different risk factors[23]. Furthermore, it can be adapted to include non-normal return distributions and capture extreme events; at the same time, however, its main disadvantage is its computational complexity, as it requires significant computing resources and accurate modelling of input parameters.

As analysed previously, each method for calculating VaR has positive and negative aspects, and for this reason, financial institutions often use a combination of these methods to obtain a more accurate estimate of VaR, balancing simplicity, speed, and precision.

Although it is a widely used measure, VaR has some limitations, including the fact that it only provides an estimate of the maximum potential loss within a certain confidence level, but cannot provide information on losses beyond that threshold. This results in a problem during extreme market events, especially in the case where the parametric method is used, which, as mentioned earlier, assumes a normal distribution of returns.

To address these limitations, investors tend to use other metrics in combination with VaR, such as Expected Shortfall (ES), which also captures losses beyond the VaR threshold, thus providing a more complete view of overall risk.

2.4.2. Alternative methods for calculating VaR

In addition to the three main methods of calculating Value at Risk (VaR) – the parametric method (variance-covariance), the historical method, and the Monte Carlo simulation method – there are also other alternative approaches to calculate VaR.

These alternative methods have been developed to address the limitations or specific requirements of investors and financial institutions, with the aim of improving the

[23] Jorion P., *Value at Risk: The New Benchmark for Managing Financial Risk*, McGraw-Hill, p. 3.

ability of VaR to capture actual risks, especially in contexts characterized by non-normal distributions, extreme events, and non-linear correlations.

One of the main alternative methods for calculating VaR is the component or Marginal VaR[24]. This metric is fundamental as it makes it possible to break down the total risk of a portfolio, allowing the contribution of each individual asset to the overall risk to be determined.

For investors, it is essential to calculate the total VaR of a portfolio, but at the same time, it is also important to understand and identify which asset or group of assets contributes most to that risk, in order to adopt appropriate management decisions.

Marginal VaR allows the measurement of changes in total VaR by changing the position of a single asset even by a small amount.

The formula for calculating the Marginal VaR for a single asset in a portfolio i is the following:

$$\text{Marginal VaR}_i = \frac{\partial \text{VaR}}{\partial w_i} \tag{15}$$

Where:

- $\frac{\partial \text{VaR}}{\partial w_i}$ represents the derivative of VaR with respect to the weight of asset i in the portfolio.

Marginal VaR is particularly useful for portfolio managers because it allows them to identify which assets increase overall risk the most and to evaluate a possible reduction in the weight of such assets in the portfolio to optimize risk management.

It is also possible to distinguish between unconditional VaR and conditional VaR; in fact, unconditional VaR is calculated without considering prevailing market conditions, with the assumption that the distribution of returns is stable over time. In contrast, conditional VaR incorporates information on specific market conditions, such as macroeconomic events or recent volatility, in order to dynamically estimate risk.

Very often, conditional VaR uses models such as the GARCH model (Generalized Autoregressive Conditional Heteroskedasticity) for a better estimation of future

---

[24] Jorion P., *Value at Risk: The New Benchmark for Managing Financial Risk*, McGraw-Hill, p. 3.

market volatility and to adjust VaR with more effective data. Given their characteristics, the conditional VaR approach is more flexible but at the same time more complex to implement compared to unconditional VaR.

Looking more specifically at the conditional VaR method and, in particular, that conditioned on the economic cycle, we can state that it is an advanced technique that considers economic cyclicality, i.e., the variations in risk levels that are identified depending on the different phases of the economic cycle (expansion, stability, and recession). This metric makes it possible to recognize that market risks are not constant but change according to the economic context. For example, during periods of recession, the risk of financial losses increases.

Implementing this type of VaR involves the use of models that combine macroeconomic variables (such as GDP, inflation, interest rates) with the portfolio structure, simulating different economic scenarios. Thanks to this approach, it is possible to obtain a more accurate VaR estimate, adaptable to the current phase of the economic cycle and more representative of actual risks.

For example, if we are in a situation of economic growth, companies tend to have positive financial results, and stock markets are positive; in this case, the VaR of an equity portfolio could be relatively low. This is because the risk of extreme losses is reduced in an expansionary context. However, it should be considered that, even in an expansionary phase, the VaR analysis could include possible volatility or unexpected events, such as a sudden rise in interest rates that could negatively affect equities.

Another case we can analyse is related to a condition of economic recession, i.e., a situation in which company profits tend to decrease, unemployment rises, and stock markets may record heavy losses; in this case, the VaR conditioned to the recession would be higher, to reflect the greater probability of significant losses. By way of example, an equity portfolio could have a VaR that is 5% higher in this phase compared to the period of economic growth, signalling a substantial increase in the risk of loss over a month.

The third case under consideration may be that related to a phase of economic recovery; in this case, markets begin to stabilize after a recession, and there is an expectation of future improvement, but there is still uncertainty, and therefore markets may remain volatile. In this phase, VaR could be higher than in the expansion phase but lower than in the recession, reflecting the risks still present.

2.5. Expected shortfall (ES)

Expected Shortfall (ES) is an advanced risk measure that extends the concept of Value at Risk (VaR), seeking to provide a more comprehensive assessment of the potential losses of a portfolio. Expected Shortfall is also known as Conditional Value at Risk (CVaR), Expected Tail Loss (ETL)[25] or Tail VaR.

The main difference between Expected Shortfall and VaR lies in the fact that VaR calculates the maximum loss that could be incurred with a certain probability, while Expected Shortfall calculates the expected average loss in particularly adverse market situations, i.e., when the VaR threshold is exceeded. The ES method is particularly important in contexts characterized by extreme events or asymmetric distributions of returns, which make VaR an insufficient measure for risk control.

Thanks to its characteristics and precision, ES has assumed fundamental importance in financial risk management, to the point of being introduced as a standard for the calculation of capital requirements for certain financial institutions under some regulations.

Expected Shortfall is defined as the average loss conditional on losses being greater than the VaR value for a given confidence level α. In short, while VaR provides a threshold under which all the most probable losses are concentrated, ES focuses on the losses that exceed that threshold.

Formally, for a confidence level α, Expected Shortfall can be expressed as:

$$\text{ES}_\alpha(X) = \mathbb{E}[\,X \mid X > \text{VaR}_\alpha(X)\,] \tag{16}$$

Where:

- X is the loss of a portfolio,
- $\text{VaR}_\alpha(X)$ is the Value at Risk at the confidence level α.

[25] Dowd K., *Measuring Market Risk*, p. 26.

Expected Shortfall can also be expressed in integral form as

$$\text{ES}_{\alpha}(X) = \frac{1}{1-\alpha}\int_{\alpha}^{1} \text{VaR}_{u}\,(X)\,du \tag{17}$$

Where:

- $\text{VaR}_u(X)$ is the Value at Risk at level u,
- α is the chosen confidence level, such as 0.95 or 0.99.

This measure therefore provides an indication of how much one can expect to lose, on average, in the worst cases.

Analysing specifically the advantages of Expected Shortfall compared to traditional VaR, we can note:

- Risk coherence, since ES is a coherent risk measure, satisfying all the properties required of risk measures, such as sub-additivity[26], which ensures that the total risk of a diversified portfolio does not exceed the sum of the risks of its components.
- Assessment of extreme losses, since ES takes into account the most severe losses, whereas VaR, as previously mentioned, ignores what happens beyond its confidence level. This feature makes ES more suitable for assessing risks in the presence of fat tails or extreme events such as those that occur during financial crises.
- A more representative measure of actual risk, because unlike VaR, which provides a risk measure based on a probability threshold, ES makes it possible to calculate a more representative measure of overall risk by identifying not only the critical loss threshold but also the amount of losses in adverse situations.

The calculation of Expected Shortfall is based on the methods used for calculating VaR, extending them to cover the specific purpose of ES. Consequently, the main methods for calculating Expected Shortfall are: the Parametric method (variance-covariance), the Historical method, and the Monte Carlo simulation method.

[26] Acerbi C., Tasche D., *On the Coherence of Expected Shortfall* in *Journal of Banking and Finance*, 2002.

Naturally, these methods have the same characteristics and potential limitations described in the section dedicated to VaR calculation.

The first method to be analysed is the Parametric method (variance-covariance), which is mainly based on the assumption of a normal distribution of returns; in this specific case, ES is calculated considering the mean and standard deviation parameters of the distribution of returns. As already mentioned, the main limitation of this approach is precisely this assumption, which does not allow for the consideration of fat tails and asymmetries present in real financial return distributions.

The formula for Expected Shortfall, in the case of normally distributed returns and confidence level α, is:

$$ES_\alpha = \mu - \sigma \frac{\phi(z_\alpha)}{1-\alpha} \tag{18}$$

Where:

- μ is the mean return of the portfolio,
- σ is the standard deviation of returns,
- $\phi(z_\alpha)$ is the density function of the standard normal distribution,
- z_α is the critical value corresponding to the confidence level α in the standard normal distribution.

The Historical method, on the other hand, is based on historical data of portfolio returns. In this case, the VaR is first calculated at the desired confidence level and then the average of the losses exceeding that threshold is considered. The Historical method is easily applicable thanks to its simplicity and the absence of distributional assumptions, but at the same time, it has a limitation related to the quality and quantity of historical data available.

The Monte Carlo simulation method allows, as already mentioned in other sections of this chapter, the generation of multiple scenarios of portfolio returns. After calculating the scenarios, VaR is computed and ES is determined as the average of the losses exceeding that threshold. This method proves to be more flexible than the previous ones and has the advantage of adapting to complex return distributions, but at the same time it also presents some critical issues, such as the high computational burden required.

Expected Shortfall is applied in numerous contexts such as financial regulations, stress tests, and risk measurement in derivative instruments and hedging strategies.

In the case of financial regulation, ES has been integrated, from a regulatory perspective, into the capital requirements of banks by the Basel Committee, as it is considered a more representative measure of risk than traditional VaR.

ES is also commonly used in stress testing and risk management, in fact it is employed to verify the resilience of a portfolio in unfavorable market conditions, thus providing an estimate of extreme losses.

Another area of application of ES is risk measurement in derivative instruments and hedging strategies, since these strategies require very precise estimates of potential losses in high-risk contexts.

CHAPTER 3

PORTFOLIO RISK MANAGEMENT

One of the fundamental aspects in the construction and monitoring of financial investments is portfolio risk management. This process aims to identify, measure, and mitigate the risks that can affect the overall return of the portfolio. As already mentioned in the previous chapters, investors use various techniques and mathematical models to try to balance the trade-off between risk and return, in order to maximize profits under conditions of uncertainty.

According to Elton et al.[27], portfolio risk is managed through an approach that includes diversification, the use of hedging strategies, and continuous control of both specific and systematic risks.

Risk management is closely linked to Modern Portfolio Theory, developed by Markowitz in 1952, according to which the expected return of a portfolio must be evaluated in relation to the risk taken.

Many scholars have analysed portfolio risk management, each with different objectives, but all agree that the key to success is to balance risk and return consistently with the investor's financial goals[28].

In this chapter, the models of Markowitz, Risk Parity, and the VaR theory will be specifically analysed, including some simple practical applications.

---

[27] Elton, E. J., Gruber M. J., Brown S. J., Goetzmann W. N., *Modern Portfolio Theory and Investment Analysis*, Wiley, 2014.

[28] Campbell, J. Y., Lo, A. W., & MacKinlay, A. C. *The Econometrics of Financial Markets*. Princeton University Press, 2001.

3.1. The Markowitz model

The Markowitz model, also known as Portfolio Theory or Efficient Diversification Theory, was developed by Harry Markowitz, an American economist and Nobel Prize winner in Economics in 1990. The model was published in 1952 and profoundly reshaped the concepts related to portfolio management. This theory laid the foundations for modern analysis of risk and return[29], proposing a quantitative and systematic approach to building efficient portfolios that maximize expected return for a given level of risk.

The fundamental intuition behind the Markowitz model is that the risk of a portfolio does not depend only on the risks of individual securities, but also on the correlation between the returns of those securities. This implies that investors can reduce the overall portfolio risk through diversification, that is, by carefully selecting securities in order to optimize the combination of risk and return.

In the Markowitz model, a portfolio is composed of a set of securities and is described in terms of expected return and risk. These two dimensions are the basis of investment decisions:

- The expected return of a portfolio, denoted as $(E(R_p))$, represents the weighted average of the expected returns of the individual securities that make up the portfolio and is determined by the following formula:

$$E(R_p) = \sum_{i=1}^{n} w_i \, E(R_i) \tag{19}$$

  Where:

  - $E(R_p)$ is the expected return of the portfolio;
  - w_i is the weight of the i-th security in the portfolio;
  - $E(R_i)$ is the expected return of the i-th security;
  - n is the number of securities in the portfolio.

- The risk of a portfolio, in the Markowitz model, is measured through the variance or the standard deviation of the portfolio returns. Unlike expected

[29] Markowitz H., *Portfolio Selection* in *Journal of Finance*, p. 3.

return, portfolio risk is not simply the weighted average of the risks of individual securities, but also depends on the correlation between their returns. Mathematically, the standard deviation of the portfolio σ_p is calculated as:

$$\sigma_p = \sqrt{\sum_{i=1}^{n}\sum_{j=1}^{n} w_i w_j Cov(R_i, R_j)} \qquad (20)$$

Where:

- σ_p is the standard deviation of the portfolio;
- $w_i w_j$ are the weights of securities i and j in the portfolio;
- $Cov(R_i, R_j)$ is the covariance between the returns of securities i and j (often represented in matrix form as Σ_{ij}).

The theory behind the Markowitz model states that through appropriate diversification, it is possible to reduce the overall risk of a portfolio without compromising its expected return. Diversification makes it possible to combine securities with returns that are not perfectly correlated, thereby reducing overall risk thanks to the balancing effect of the movements of individual securities.

It is therefore possible to create an efficient portfolio, that is, a portfolio offering the maximum expected return for a given level of risk. The efficient frontier is defined by Markowitz as the set of portfolios that cannot be improved in terms of risk and return[30].

[30] Sharpe, W. F., *Capital Asset Prices: A Theory of Market Equilibrium Under Conditions of Risk* in *Journal of Finance*, p. 23.

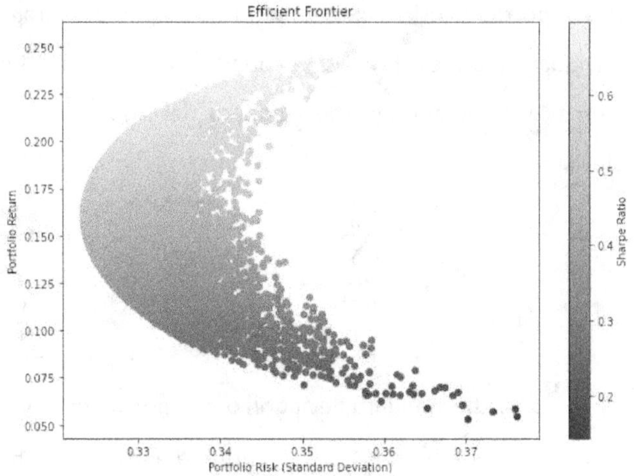

Figure 2 – Efficient Frontier[31]

This concept is well represented by the curve of the efficient frontier, which plots the relationship between risk and return for all optimal portfolios. On the efficient frontier curve, each point represents a portfolio with an optimal combination of risk and return. The concave shape of the efficient frontier reflects the principle of diversification: it is possible to reduce risk by combining securities with low or negative correlations, without sacrificing expected return.

Portfolios located on the efficient frontier are considered optimal, as they provide the best trade-off between risk and return. Conversely, portfolios that lie below the efficient frontier are non-optimal, because there exist portfolios that offer higher returns with the same level of risk, or lower risk for the same level of return.

In the Markowitz model, one of the fundamental elements is the risk-return trade-off. One of the first decisions investors must make is the level of risk they are willing to assume in exchange for a higher expected return. Depending on the intrinsic characteristics of the investor, they will position themselves differently along the frontier: risk-seeking investors will choose portfolios in the upper part of the frontier, where expected return is higher (but risk is also greater), while risk-averse investors will opt for portfolios located in the lower part of the efficient frontier, where risk is lower but expected return is more modest.

[31] Colombo M., *Strategic Adjustment and Quantitative Risk Management*, 2024.

The Markowitz model also introduced the Capital Market Line (CML), which represents the optimal portfolio in the presence of a risk-free rate, such as a government bond. This concept was later expanded upon by William Sharpe. The CML is the straight-line tangent to the efficient frontier, starting from the point that represents the risk-free asset; its slope represents the ratio between the excess return obtained and the additional risk assumed (also called the risk premium).
The equation of the CML is as follows:

$$E(R_p) = R_f + \frac{E(R_m) - R_f}{\sigma_m} \cdot \sigma_p \tag{21}$$

Where:

- $E(R_p)$ is the expected return of the portfolio;
- R_f is the risk-free rate;
- $E(R_m)$ is the expected return of the market portfolio;
- σ_m is the standard deviation of the market (i.e., market risk);
- σ_p is the standard deviation of the portfolio (the total portfolio risk, measured as volatility).

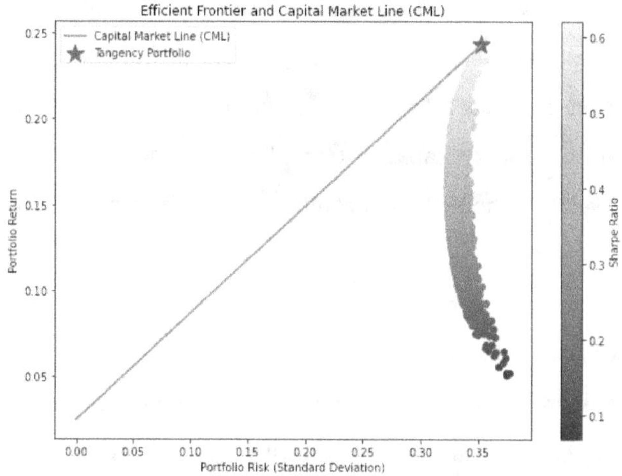

Figure 3 – Efficient Frontier and Capital Market Line (CML)[32]

This equation shows that the expected return of a portfolio, $E(R_p)$ is composed of the risk-free rate, R_f, and a risk premium proportional to the portfolio's own risk (σ_p),

[32] Colombo M., *Strategic Adjustment and Quantitative Risk Management*, p. 37.

with a coefficient equal to the ratio between the market risk premium ($E(R_m) - R_f$) and the market risk (σ_m).

Based on their positioning relative to the CML, three types of portfolios can be identified:

- Portfolios below the CML are inefficient, because for the same level of risk there exist portfolios that offer a higher expected return.
- Portfolios on the CML are efficient, as they provide the maximum expected return for a given level of risk. These portfolios are optimal combinations of a risky portfolio (the market portfolio) and the risk-free asset. The slope of the CML represents the optimal Sharpe ratio.

$$\text{Indice di Sharpe} = \frac{E(R_P) - R_f}{\sigma_P} \tag{22}$$

Where:

- $E(R_P)$ is the expected return of the portfolio;
- R_f is the risk-free rate;
- σ_P is the standard deviation of the portfolio.

- The tangent portfolio is the market portfolio, identified by the tangent point between the CML and the efficient frontier (which represents only risky portfolios). This portfolio contains all risky assets weighted according to their market capitalization. All rational investors, regardless of their risk aversion, should hold a combination of the market portfolio and the risk-free asset.

However, it should be noted that the Markowitz model, despite its relevance, presents some limitations:

The model assumes that asset returns follow a normal distribution, which may not accurately reflect financial market realities; in fact, in the presence of extreme events or "fat tails" in the return distribution, the model may underestimate actual risks.

The model uses variance or standard deviation as the sole measure of risk, while many investors are more concerned with potential losses (downside risk) than overall volatility. For this reason, more advanced models, such as Value at Risk (VaR) or Expected Shortfall (ES), are often used to capture risks more focused on losses.

The model requires the estimation of numerous parameters, including expected returns, variances, and covariances between securities. However, these estimates are based on historical data, which may not accurately reflect future market conditions, making the model sensitive to estimation errors[33].

Another assumption of the Markowitz model is the existence of perfect markets, with no transaction costs, taxes, or investment constraints. In practice, however, these factors can significantly influence portfolio construction.

3.1.1. Construction of an optimal portfolio

To clarify the mechanism of constructing a portfolio based on the Markowitz model, this section presents an empirical application of the theory, retracing the main stages in portfolio creation.

Let us imagine building an equity portfolio composed of three securities, A, B, and C, for which we know the expected returns, the standard deviations, and the correlations.

Title	Expected Return ($E(R_i)$)	Standard Deviation (σ_i)
Asset A	0.08	0.15
Asset B	0.10	0.20
Asset C	0.12	0.25

Table 1 – Expected Returns and Standard Deviation[34]

The first step in applying the Markowitz model is to calculate the correlation matrix.

	Asset A	Asset B	Asset C
Asset A	1.00	0.50	0.30
Asset B	0.50	1.00	0.40
Asset C	0.30	0.40	1.00

Table 2 – Correlation Matrix Values[35]

After calculating the correlation, the next step is to obtain the covariance matrix $\text{Cov}(R_i, R_j)$:

$$\text{Cov}(R_i, R_j) = \rho_{ij} \cdot \sigma_i \cdot \sigma_j = \Sigma_{ij} \tag{23}$$

[33] Elton, E. J., Gruber M. J., Brown S. J., Goetzmann W. N., *Modern Portfolio Theory and Investment Analysis*, p. 35.

[34] Author's own elaboration

[35] Author's own elaboration

Applying the above formula for the calculation of the covariance matrix, we obtain:

- $\Sigma = \begin{bmatrix} 0.0225 & 0.015 & 0.01125 \\ 0.015 & 0.04 & 0.02 \\ 0.01125 & 0.02 & 0.0625 \end{bmatrix}$

After computing the covariance matrix, we calculate the expected portfolio return $E(R_p)$, applying formula (19), initially assuming that the asset weights are equal $(w_A = w_B = w_C = 1/3)$:

- $E(R_p) = 1/3 \cdot 0.08 + 1/3 \cdot 0.10 + 1/3 \cdot 0.12 = 0.10 = 10\%$

Now we calculate the variance and the standard deviation of the portfolio, respectively using formulas (5) and (20).

The variance, substituting the values, will be equal to:

- $\sigma_p^2 = (1/3)^2 \cdot 0.0225 + (1/3)^2 \cdot 0.04 + (1/3)^2 \cdot 0.0625 + 2 \cdot (1/3)^2 \cdot (0.015 + 0.01125 + 0.02)$
- $\sigma_p^2 = 0.0075 + 0.0133 + 0.0208 + 2 \cdot 0.0151 = 0.0718$

In this case, since the variance has already been computed, instead of using relation (20) for the calculation of the standard deviation, it is more convenient to use the relation that links variance and standard deviation, already cited in previous sections, which can be expressed mathematically as:

$$\sigma_p = \sqrt{\sigma_p^2} \tag{24}$$

Thus, substituting the data into the formula, we obtain:

- $\sigma_p = \sqrt{0.0718} = 0.268 = 26.8\%$

We now move on to the most important phase, namely optimization. To optimize the weights, we use the constraint of minimizing risk for a given expected return. This implies solving the following quadratic programming problem:

$$\min_{w} w^T \Sigma w \quad \text{subject to} \quad \sum_{i=1}^{n} w_i = 1 \quad \text{and} \quad E(R_p) = R_t \tag{25}$$

where R_t is the target return. Let us set, for example, $R_t = 10\%$. To solve this system, tools such as Excel Solver, Python, or Matlab can be used. The optimized result produces weights that minimize risk for an expected return of 10%:

- $w_A = 0.40, \quad w_B = 0.35, \quad w_C = 0.25$

Now, the optimal portfolio with the optimized weights presents an expected return and standard deviation equal to:

- $E(R_p) = 0.40 \cdot 0.08 + 0.35 \cdot 0.10 + 0.25 \cdot 0.12 = 0.10 = 10\%$
- $\sigma_p = 0.224 = 22.4\%$

In conclusion, thanks to the Markowitz model, it was possible to create a portfolio that minimizes risk for a fixed expected return. This approach allows investors to balance risk and return in a systematic and efficient manner.

3.2. Risk Parity method

One of the most innovative approaches used in portfolio construction is the Risk Parity method; it is characterized by the balanced distribution of risk among the different components of the portfolio. The fundamental principle on which this method is based lies in the idea that the total risk of a portfolio should not be dominated by a single asset or asset class, but should instead be equally divided among all its components, in order to achieve greater stability and resilience under different market scenarios.

The principle of Risk Parity develops from the concept of Marginal Risk, which defines and measures the contribution to total risk made by each individual asset within the portfolio. This contribution takes into account both the individual volatility of the assets and the correlations between them. The main purpose of this method is to achieve a risk-balanced allocation, such that each asset contributes equally to the overall risk of the portfolio.

3.2.1. Risk Parity theory

The Risk Parity theory was born out of the need to overcome the limitations of traditional portfolio allocation models, which rely on estimates of expected returns and variances. Risk Parity, instead, focuses specifically on the distribution of risk, seeking to balance it among the different components of the portfolio.

Mathematically, the Risk Parity formula in marginal terms is:

$$\frac{\partial \sigma_p}{\partial w_i} \cdot w_i = \frac{\partial \sigma_p}{\partial w_j} \cdot w_j \quad \forall\, i,j \tag{26}$$

Where:

- σ_p is the total risk of the portfolio (often measured as the standard deviation of portfolio returns, or another risk measure).
- w_i and w_j are the weights of assets i and j in the portfolio.
- $\frac{\partial \sigma_p}{\partial w_i}$ is the marginal contribution to risk of asset i.

To correctly develop the concept of Risk Parity, one must know the total portfolio risk σ_p, which is calculated using the following formula:

$$\sigma_p = \sqrt{w^{\top} \Sigma w} \tag{27}$$

Where:

- w is the vector of asset weights.
- Σ is the covariance matrix of asset returns.

In addition to the formula mentioned above, for the calculation of the Marginal Risk Contribution (MRC) there is also a more precise formula, which allows one to take into account the entire portfolio and the relationships among assets, although it is more complex to apply. This formula is particularly relevant when the covariance matrix (Σ) is known.

Mathematically, the formula is as follows:

$$MRC_i = \frac{\partial \sigma_p}{\partial w_i} = \sum_{j=1}^{n} \Sigma_{ij} \cdot w_j \tag{28}$$

Where:

- Σ_{ij}: the element of the covariance matrix representing the covariance between assets i and j.
- w_j: the weight of asset j in the portfolio.

To calculate the contribution of an asset to portfolio risk (RC), two different formulas can be used, depending on whether one is interested in the absolute or relative risk contribution.

In the case of absolute risk contribution of asset *i*, the following formula is applied:

$$RC_i = w_i \cdot MRC_i \tag{29}$$

Where:

- w_i is the weight of asset i in the portfolio.
- MRC_i is the marginal risk of asset i, i.e., the change in total portfolio risk resulting from a small increase in the weight of i.

To correctly calculate the relative risk contribution of asset i, expressed as a fraction (or percentage) of the total portfolio risk (σ_p), the following formula is applied:

$$RC_i = \frac{w_i \cdot MRC_i}{\sigma_p} \tag{30}$$

Where:

- w_i is the weight of asset i in the portfolio,
- MRC_i is the Marginal Risk Contribution of asset i,
- σ_p is the total portfolio risk.

The principle of Risk Parity implies that RC_i must be equal for all assets included in the portfolio.

One of the main favourable aspects that distinguishes Risk Parity from other approaches is the fact that this method does not require estimates of expected returns, thereby eliminating an important source of uncertainty in the decision-making process. Precisely for this reason, it is particularly useful in contexts where future returns are difficult to predict or highly volatile. Another advantage of Risk Parity lies in the fact that, unlike equal-weighted portfolios, it takes into account differences in the risk characteristics of assets, such as volatility and correlation, thus providing a more sophisticated and balanced allocation[36].

Despite its usefulness and advantages, the Risk Parity theory is not free from limitations. The main limitations of this theory lie in its dependence on the covariance matrix, which can be unstable or subject to changes over time, and in the fact that it does not explicitly consider expected returns. This latter aspect is advantageous in terms of reducing estimation issues, but at the same time it may lead to overlooking investment opportunities with potentially high returns and reduced risk.

[36] Qian, E., *Risk Parity Portfolios: Efficient and Diversified*, PanAgora Asset Management, 2011.

The Risk Parity theory has had a significant influence on risk management and capital allocation. One of the main areas where this theory is applied is in multi-asset portfolios, where it allows risks of different natures to be balanced, such as those related to equities, bonds, and commodities. This theory is also applied in institutional contexts to create more resilient portfolios that are less sensitive to adverse macroeconomic conditions[37].

3.2.2. Construction of an optimal portfolio

To clarify the mechanism of constructing a portfolio based on the Risk Parity theory, this paragraph proposes an empirical application, retracing the main stages of portfolio creation. Let us imagine having three hypothetical assets, A, B, and C. Suppose we know the following data regarding their expected returns and historical volatility.

Asset	Standard Deviation (σ)	Correlation with A	Correlation with B	Correlation with C
A	0,15	1	0,3	0,5
B	0,1	0,3	1	0,2
C	0,2	0,5	0,2	1

Table 3 – Standard Deviation and Asset Correlation[38]

As already introduced in the theoretical section, the objective of the Risk Parity method is to construct a portfolio with weights (w_a, w_b, w_c) such that the relative risk contribution of each asset is equal.

The first step in applying the Risk Parity method is to calculate the covariance matrix (Σ), using formula (23).

	Asset A (σ_a)	Asset B (σ_b)	Asset C (σ_c)
Asset A	0.0225	0.0045	0.015
Asset B	0.0045	0.01	0.004
Asset C	0.015	0.004	0.04

Table 4 – Covariance Matrix Values[39]

[37] Asness, C. S., Frazzini, A., Pedersen, L. H., *Leverage Aversion and Risk Parity*, in *Financial Analysts Journal*, 2012, No.1.

[38] Author's own elaboration

[39] Author's own elaboration

The resulting matrix is:

- $\Sigma = \begin{bmatrix} 0.0225 & 0.0045 & 0.015 \\ 0.0045 & 0.01 & 0.004 \\ 0.015 & 0.004 & 0.04 \end{bmatrix}$

After calculating the covariance matrix (Σ), the second step consists of computing the marginal risk for each asset MRC_i. In this case, we will use formula (24), introduced in the previous section. Before calculating the MRC, we start with an initial estimate of the weights: $w_a = w_b = w_c = 1/3 = 0.3333$. We then calculate the marginal risk (MRC_i) for each asset using formula (28):

- Asset A: $MRC_a = 0.0225 \cdot 0.3333 + 0.0045 \cdot 0.3333 + 0.015 \cdot 0.3333 = 0.0075 + 0.0015 + 0.005 = 0.014$
- Asset B: $MRC_b = 0.0045 \cdot 0.3333 + 0.01 \cdot 0.3333 + 0.004 \cdot 0.3333 = 0.0015 + 0.0033 + 0.0013 = 0.0061$
- Asset C: $MRC_c = 0.015 \cdot 0.3333 + 0.004 \cdot 0.3333 + 0.04 \cdot 0.3333 = 0.005 + 0.0013 + 0.0133 = 0.0196$

The next step is to calculate the absolute risk contribution (RC_i) of each asset using formula (29).

- Asset A: $RC_a = 0.3333 \cdot 0.014 = 0.00467$
- Asset B: $RC_b = 0.3333 \cdot 0.0061 = 0.00203$
- Asset C: $RC_c = 0.3333 \cdot 0.0196 = 0.00653$

After calculating the risk contributions (RC_i), the weights must be adjusted to achieve risk parity, that is, to obtain $RC_a = RC_b = RC_c$.

To correctly calculate the Target RC (Average risk contribution), which represents a theoretical benchmark used in the Risk Parity method, we use the following formula:

$$\text{Target RC} = \frac{\text{Total portfolio risk } (\sigma_p)}{n} \tag{31}$$

Obviously, before calculating the Target RC, we must compute the total portfolio risk (σ_p) using formula (20). Using the initial weights $w_a = w_b = w_c = 0.3333$, we obtain:

- $\sigma_p^2 = (0.3333)^2(0.0225) + (0.3333)^2(0.01) + (0.3333)^2(0.04) + 2(0.3333^2)(0.0045) + 2(0.3333^2)(0.015) + 2(0.3333^2)(0.004)$

Simplifying:

- $\sigma_p^2 = 0.0025 + 0.0011 + 0.0044 + 0.0009 + 0.0033 + 0.0009 = 0.0131$

Therefore, applying relation (24):

- $\sigma_p = \sqrt{0.0131} = 0.1144$, ovvero, 11,44%.

Now the average risk contribution is:

- Target RC $= 0.1144/3 = 0.0381$

We update the weights w_i using the following formula:

$$w_i^{(new)} = w_i^{(old)} \cdot \frac{\text{Target RC}}{RC_i} \tag{32}$$

- Asset A: $w_a^{(new)} = 0.3333 \cdot 0.0381/0.00467 = 0.3333 \cdot 8.16 = 2.72$
- Asset B: $w_b^{(new)} = 0.3333 \cdot 0.0381/0.00203 = 0.3333 \cdot 18.77 = 6.25$
- Asset C: $w_c^{(new)} = 0.3333 \cdot 0.0381/0.00653 = 0.3333 \cdot 5.83 = 1.94$

After calculating the new weights, they must be normalized, since the sum of the new weights must equal 1. We divide each weight by the total sum ("Total weights" = 2.72+6.25+1.94=10.91).

- Asset A: $w_a = 2.72/10.91 = 0.2494$
- Asset B: $w_b = 6.25/10.91 = 0.5730$
- Asset C: $w_c = 1.94/10.91 = 0.1776$

Now, with the normalized weights, we recalculate the risk contributions RC_iusing formula (29).

- Asset A: $RC_a = 0.2494 \cdot 0.014 = 0.00349$
- Asset B: $RC_b = 0.5730 \cdot 0.0061 = 0.00349$
- Asset C: $RC_c = 0.1776 \cdot 0.0196 = 0.00349$

We then verify that the contributions are equal:

- $RC_a = RC_b = RC_c = 0.00349$

The contributions are equal, which means that risk parity has been achieved.

In conclusion, the optimal portfolio weights that satisfy the Risk Parity criterion are:

- $w_a = 0.2494,\ w_b = 0.5730,\ w_c = 0.1776$

3.3. VaR method

The Value at Risk (VaR) method, already widely discussed from a theoretical perspective in section 2.4, is one of the main tools for portfolio risk management. Its importance lies in the fact that it provides a synthetic measure of the potential loss under normal market conditions, within a given confidence interval and over a specific time horizon. From the perspective of active portfolio management, the VaR method is not only used to quantify overall risk, but also as a guide for asset allocation decisions and the optimization of portfolio structure.

3.3.1. Theory of VaR

In the previous chapters, VaR and its main estimation methods were analyzed in detail. In this section, the key steps for estimating the VaR of a portfolio will be introduced, before presenting a practical example in section 3.3.2.

The first step in constructing a portfolio optimized through the VaR method is to define the basic parameters of VaR, such as:

- Time horizon (T): the period over which the risk is assessed;
- Confidence level (α): the probability with which the maximum loss is estimated;
- Risk tolerance threshold: the maximum acceptable level of VaR for the investor.

Once the base parameters have been defined, it is necessary to calculate the VaR for each asset in the portfolio using the following formula:

$$VaR_i = \Phi^{-1}(\alpha) \cdot \sigma_i \cdot \sqrt{T} \cdot w_i \qquad (33)$$

Where:

- $\Phi^{-1}(\alpha)$ is the inverse quantile of the normal distribution associated with the confidence level α;
- σ_i is the volatility of asset i;
- w_i is the weight of asset i in the portfolio;
- T is the time horizon considered.

Next, the overall portfolio VaR must be calculated. This is not simply the sum of the individual asset VaRs, but also takes into account the correlation between assets, through the covariance matrix Σ:

$$VaR_p = \Phi^{-1}(\alpha) \cdot \sqrt{w^T \Sigma w} \qquad (34)$$

Where:

- w is the vector of asset weights in the portfolio;
- Σ is the covariance matrix of returns.

A further key step is portfolio optimization. The goal of this procedure is to optimize the asset weights (w_i) in order to minimize the overall VaR (VaR_p), while simultaneously satisfying potential constraints on expected return and risk tolerance. Mathematically, the constrained minimization problem can be expressed as:

$$\min_{w} VaR_p \quad \text{subject to:} \tag{35}$$

- $\sum_{i=1}^{n} w_i = 1$ weights sum to 100% of the portfoli
- $R_p = \sum_{i=1}^{n} w_i \cdot \mu_i \geq R_{target}$ (minimum expected return);
- $w_i \geq 0$ (no short-selling, if required).

This problem can be solved using numerical techniques such as quadratic programming.

Following the process described above, the construction of a portfolio using the VaR method can be carried out. However, the resulting portfolio must be periodically monitored to ensure that the overall VaR remains within the established risk limits. In practice, portfolio rebalancing often becomes necessary whenever there are significant changes in market conditions, returns, or correlations among assets.

3.3.2. Construction of an optimal portfolio

After having described, from a theoretical perspective in section (3.3.1), the procedure for building an optimal portfolio through the VaR method, a practical application is now presented.

Let us consider, for example, a portfolio composed of three assets A, B, and C, with the following parameters.

Asset	Expected Return (R_i)	Volatility (σ_i)	Initial Weight (w_i)
A	8%	15%	0,4
B	6%	10%	0,3
C	10%	20%	0,3

Table 5 – Expected Returns, Volatility and Initial Weights

By calculating the correlation matrix among the assets, we obtain:

- $\rho_{ij} = \begin{bmatrix} 1.00 & 0.80 & 0.50 \\ 0.80 & 1.00 & 0.40 \\ 0.50 & 0.40 & 1.00 \end{bmatrix}$

Using the values from the correlation matrix and the volatilities (σ_i), we derive the covariance matrix (Σ) through formula (23):

- $\Sigma = \begin{bmatrix} 0.0225 & 0.012 & 0.015 \\ 0.012 & 0.010 & 0.008 \\ 0.015 & 0.008 & 0.040 \end{bmatrix}$

After calculating these necessary values for the subsequent steps, we compute the overall portfolio VaR using formula (34), restated here:

$$VaR_p = \Phi^{-1}(\alpha) \cdot \sqrt{w^T \Sigma w}$$

Where:

- $\Phi^{-1}(\alpha)$: the inverse quantile of the normal distribution (for a 95% confidence level, $\Phi^{-1}(0.95) = 1.645$);
- w^T: the transposed weight vector ($[0.4,0.3,0.3]$).

We now compute the term $w^T \Sigma w$:

- $w^T \Sigma w = [0.4,0.3,0.3] \cdot \begin{bmatrix} 0.0225 & 0.012 & 0.015 \\ 0.012 & 0.010 & 0.008 \\ 0.015 & 0.008 & 0.040 \end{bmatrix} \cdot \begin{bmatrix} 0.4 \\ 0.3 \\ 0.3 \end{bmatrix}$

Carrying out the partial calculations, we first multiply Σ by w, then compute the scalar product $w^T \cdot (\Sigma \cdot w)$:

- $\Sigma \cdot w = \begin{bmatrix} 0.0225 & 0.012 & 0.015 \\ 0.012 & 0.010 & 0.008 \\ 0.015 & 0.008 & 0.040 \end{bmatrix} \cdot \begin{bmatrix} 0.4 \\ 0.3 \\ 0.3 \end{bmatrix} = \begin{bmatrix} 0.0132 \\ 0.0090 \\ 0.0179 \end{bmatrix}$
- $w^T \cdot \begin{bmatrix} 0.0132 \\ 0.0090 \\ 0.0179 \end{bmatrix} = (0.4 \cdot 0.0132) + (0.3 \cdot 0.0090) + (0.3 \cdot 0.0179) =$

  0.00932

Thus, we obtain $w^T \Sigma w = 0.00932$. Having all the necessary values, we can now calculate the VaR:

- $VaR_p = 1.645 \cdot \sqrt{0.00932} = 1.645 \cdot 0.0966 = 0.1588\ (15.88\%)$

Having calculated the overall VaR of the portfolio with the three assets A, B, and C, we now set the objective of rebalancing the portfolio so that the total VaR is minimized, while simultaneously meeting the constraint of a minimum expected return, for example $R_{target} = 7\%$.

We first check the expected return of the current portfolio using formula (19):

- $R_p = (0.4 \cdot 0.08) + (0.3 \cdot 0.06) + (0.3 \cdot 0.10) = 0.078\ (7.8\%)$

Next, we minimize the VaR through an optimization model (there are several algorithms available, such as Karush-Kuhn-Tucker (KKT)), subject to the following constraints:

- $R_p \geq R_{target} = 7\%;$
- $\Sigma w_i = 1;$
- $w_i \geq 0$ (no short selling, if required).

After optimizing the initial portfolio, we obtain the following new optimal weights:

- $w_A = 0.35,\ w_B = 0.40,\ w_C = 0.25$

With the new weights, we recalculate the expected return and the overall VaR, which result in:

- $R_p = (0.35 \cdot 0.08) + (0.40 \cdot 0.06) + (0.25 \cdot 0.10) = 0.074\ (7.4\%)$
- $VaR_p = 1.645 \cdot \sqrt{w_{new}^T \Sigma w_{new}} = 1.645 \cdot \sqrt{0.0087} = 0.1535\ (15.35\%)$

We can therefore conclude that, through the VaR method, the optimized portfolio reduces overall risk, as the VaR decreases from 15.88% to 15.35%, while maintaining an adequate expected return of 7.4%. This method allows the construction of portfolios that are consciously balanced in terms of risk-return, as opposed to methods based solely on standard deviation or other risk indicators.

FINAL REMARKS AND FUTURE OUTLOOK IN PORTFOLIO RISK MANAGEMENT

Portfolio risk management is one of the most significant challenges of modern finance, with crucial implications for both investors and financial operators. The aim of this work was to examine in depth the main methodologies and tools used to measure and manage risk, while also analyzing in detail the theoretical models, their strengths and limitations, as well as their practical applications in building optimized portfolios according to risk–return preferences.

The analyses and studies presented here clearly highlight that portfolio risk management is an essential aspect for ensuring effective and rational financial decisions, especially in today's global context, characterized by volatility, uncertainty, and economic instability. Diversification alone—though it remains the cornerstone principle of risk management—must be complemented with both quantitative and qualitative analysis, leveraging advanced theoretical models and practical tools.

It has become evident that multidimensional approaches are necessary; no single model can fully capture the complexity of financial markets. Traditional methods, such as Markowitz's model and variance analysis, provide investors with a solid theoretical foundation and an introduction to understanding the risk–return relationship. However, they often prove insufficient in the face of extreme events such as financial crises or abrupt market shifts. To address these limitations, more advanced approaches—such as the Risk Parity model or the use of Value at Risk (VaR)—allow for a more dynamic and resilient form of risk management.

Through the analysis, it was observed that the Risk Parity method represents a tool capable of balancing the risk contribution equally across portfolio assets, thereby enabling the creation of more stable portfolios, regardless of market fluctuations. At the same time, VaR proved to be fundamental for identifying and managing potential losses in adverse economic scenarios. To achieve even more precise and reliable results, Conditional VaR is employed, offering a more realistic view of risk by taking into account economic variables and asset-specific volatility.

Another element of reflection concerns the role of investors' risk aversion, addressed in the first chapter. In order to construct tailored portfolios, it is essential to understand investors' preferences toward risk. At the same time, however, this part of the research has revealed that metrics based solely on utility functions or risk aversion are not sufficient in complex contexts, and must be combined with quantitative models that better capture the complexity of financial markets.

This study has also made it explicit that risk management is not a static process but rather a dynamic activity that requires constant adjustments in response to changes in the economic and financial environment. A manager's ability lies not only in the choice of sophisticated tools but also in the skill of adapting strategies to market conditions, investor objectives, and constraints.

Despite all the progress made in portfolio risk management, several limitations remain that call for further research and improvement. One of the most significant concerns the reliance on historical data. Most of the models analyzed—such as Beta, VaR, and Markowitz's framework—share the assumption that past data can be used as a proxy for the future. Yet, as emphasized throughout this work, financial markets are inherently dynamic, and economic, political, and social conditions can change rapidly, making historical data less reliable as an indicator for future investment strategies. This limitation is particularly critical in times of crisis or exogenous shocks, when historical models tend to underestimate risk.

At the same time, many models, such as traditional VaR and variance, assume a normal distribution of returns—an assumption that does not always reflect the reality of financial markets. This study has shown that markets are often characterized by asymmetric distributions with fat tails, which capture extreme events such as speculative bubbles. In such cases, more advanced tools like Expected Shortfall (ES) can better address these aspects, although they also require higher technical expertise and greater computational power.

The static approach embedded in many models is another limitation. For example, even Markowitz's model assumes that correlations between assets remain stable over time, while in reality they may change significantly depending on market conditions. This issue is also present in the Risk Parity model, which, although improving diversification, is still based on assumptions that may not hold during periods of crisis or heightened volatility.

Portfolio risk management is a continuously evolving process. Looking to the future, the increasing availability of big data, along with advances in artificial intelligence (AI) and machine learning (ML), will offer promising opportunities to enhance risk management. By employing predictive algorithms, it may become possible to anticipate changes in asset correlations, detect risk signals, and adapt strategies more dynamically. Advanced quantitative analysis tools, such as enhanced Monte Carlo simulations or neural networks, would allow for more effective management of extreme risks by more accurately capturing the complex dynamics of markets.

At the same time, the growing emphasis on sustainability in investments could open up new perspectives in risk management. The integration of ESG (environmental, social, and governance) factors into portfolios not only responds to the rising demand from investors but could also serve as a strategy to mitigate long-term risks associated with climate change or geopolitical instability.

In conclusion, despite the importance of the theoretical and practical foundations of current risk management models, today's ever-changing environment demands continuous updates of tools and strategies. A combination of emerging technologies, dynamic approaches, and greater attention to the qualitative aspects of investments will prove essential in facing future challenges and in ensuring more resilient and sustainable portfolios.

GLOSSARY

A

Allocation: Allocation is the distribution of capital among different assets or investments, based on risk and return objectives.

ARA (Absolute Risk Aversion): ARA is the index that measures how risk-averse an individual is in absolute terms relative to their wealth.

ARCH (Autoregressive Conditional Heteroskedasticity): ARCH is a conditional volatility model that allows variance to change over time depending on past errors, and is used to forecast non-constant risk dynamics.

B

Beta (β): Beta is the ratio between the covariance of an asset's return with the market and the market variance; it measures sensitivity to systematic risk.

Big data: Big data refers to large volumes of heterogeneous data which, when properly analyzed (e.g., using AI/ML), can improve risk forecasting and the optimization of financial strategies.

Black swans: Black swans are extreme and unpredictable events (such as sudden financial crises) that have a major impact on markets and are generally overlooked by traditional quantitative models.

C

Capital Asset Pricing Model (CAPM): The CAPM is a financial model that describes the relationship between systematic risk and expected returns of assets, particularly stocks. It is widely used to estimate the cost of equity.

Capital Market Line (CML): The CML is a line representing the optimal combination of the market portfolio and the risk-free asset, maximizing the risk premium (Sharpe Ratio) on the risk–return plane.

Conditional VaR: Conditional VaR is an extension of traditional VaR that incorporates dynamic variables.

Confidence interval: A confidence interval is a range of values derived from data that, with a given level of confidence (e.g., 95%), is likely to contain the true population parameter.

Correlation: Correlation is a statistical measure that shows the degree to which two assets move in relation to one another. A positive correlation means they move in the same direction, while a negative correlation means they move in opposite directions.

Correlation matrix: A correlation matrix is a table showing the correlation coefficients among several assets. It helps to understand asset relationships and is used in portfolio optimization.

Covariance: Covariance measures how two variables vary together. In finance, it is used to assess how the returns of two assets move relative to each other, contributing to portfolio diversification.
covariances between returns of all portfolio assets; it is used to calculate total risk.

Covariance matrix (Σ): The covariance matrix is a matrix collecting.

D

Distribution: In finance and statistics, distribution refers to how values—such as returns, prices, or other data—are spread across a range.

Diversification (Portfolio): Diversification is a risk mitigation technique that involves investing in different assets to reduce the impact of negative events affecting a single one.

Dynamic portfolio allocation: Dynamic portfolio allocation is a strategy in which the investor periodically adjusts the composition of assets according to market performance, risk tolerance, and other external factors.

E

Efficient Frontier: The efficient frontier is a line on the risk–return graph representing the set of optimal portfolios that provide the highest expected return for a given risk level. Portfolios on the efficient frontier are considered well-diversified.

EWMA (Exponentially Weighted Moving Average): EWMA is a model that estimates volatility by assigning exponentially greater weights to more recent data, useful when variance changes rapidly.

Expected return (μ): Expected return is the average of anticipated returns; it is used as a parameter in variance and VaR calculations.

Expected Shortfall (ES): Expected Shortfall is a coherent risk measure that estimates the average loss in the worst scenarios (beyond the VaR threshold).

G

GARCH (Generalized ARCH): GARCH is the evolution of the ARCH model, incorporating autoregressive dependence of variance; it captures phenomena such as "volatility clustering."

H

Hedging: Hedging is a risk management strategy used to offset potential losses on an investment by taking an opposite position in a related asset.

Historical volatility: Historical volatility measures past price fluctuations of an asset over a specific period. It is calculated as the standard deviation of returns.

I

Information flows: Information flows are the transmission of data and news between market actors, which can rapidly affect prices and volatility.

L

Liquidity: Liquidity refers to the ease with which an asset can be bought or sold in the market without significantly affecting its price.

Liquidity risk: Liquidity risk is the risk that an asset cannot be bought or sold quickly enough in the market without significantly affecting its price.

M

Machine Learning (ML): Machine Learning is a subset of AI that enables models to learn from data to predict risks, detect fraud, or adapt strategies.

Marginal VaR: Marginal VaR measures the contribution to total VaR resulting from a small change in the weight of an asset in the portfolio.

Market risk: Market risk refers to the possibility of losses due to factors affecting the overall performance of financial markets.

Markowitz model: The Markowitz model is a mathematical framework for portfolio optimization, introduced by Harry Markowitz in 1952.

Modern portfolio theory: Modern Portfolio Theory is an investment model that emphasizes diversification.

Monte Carlo method: The Monte Carlo method is a statistical technique that uses random sampling to model the probability of different outcomes.

N

Normal distribution: The normal distribution is a statistical distribution in which data are symmetrically distributed around the mean, forming a bell curve. In finance, it is used to model returns and assess probabilities.

P

Portfolio expected return: Portfolio expected return is the weighted average of the expected returns of individual assets.

Portfolio management: Portfolio management is the strategic process of selecting, monitoring, and adjusting a portfolio of investments to balance risk and return in line with the investor's goals.

Q

Quantitative methods: Quantitative methods are analysis techniques based on mathematics, statistics, and algorithms.

R

Risk aversion: Risk aversion refers to an investor's attitude toward outcome variability: risk-averse individuals prefer less uncertain assets, foregoing potential gains to reduce exposure.

Risk aversion: Risk aversion refers to an investor's preference for less uncertainty.

Risk Parity: Risk Parity is an allocation strategy that distributes risk equally across portfolio components.

Risk: Risk is the variability of expected returns: the more an investment fluctuates, the greater its inherent risk.

Risk–return trade-off: The risk–return trade-off is the principle that higher returns are typically associated with higher risk.

S

Sector: An economic sector refers to a broad segment of the economy composed of companies and industries with similar business activities.

Sharpe ratio: The Sharpe ratio is a performance measure that expresses the excess return relative to the risk-free rate, per unit of standard deviation.

Specific risk: Specific risk refers to the risk tied to factors of a particular stock or sector.

Standard deviation (σ): Standard deviation is the square root of variance, measuring the dispersion of returns around the mean; it is central in risk assessment.

Systematic risk: Systematic risk refers to the portion of risk related to macroeconomic factors.

T

Tangency portfolio: The tangency portfolio is the portfolio at the point of tangency between the CML and the efficient frontier.

Total risk: Total risk is the combination of systematic and specific risk

Traditional risk matrix: The traditional risk matrix is a tool combining standard deviation and Beta to compare the risk and return of assets within a portfolio.

U

Utility curve: The utility curve is a graph representing utility levels relative to risk (or wealth); it is concave for risk-averse individuals, linear for risk-neutral ones, and convex for risk-seeking individuals.

Utility theory: Utility theory explains individual behavior under uncertainty.

V

Value at Risk (VaR): VaR is a risk management measure that estimates the maximum potential portfolio loss.

Variance (σ^2): Variance is the average of the squared deviations of returns from the mean.

Volatility: Volatility is the measure of return dispersion around the mean.

LIST OF FIGURES

LIST OF TABLES

BIBLIOGRAPHY

Journal Articles

Acerbi, C., Tasche, D. (2002). *On the Coherence of Expected Shortfall.* Journal of Banking and Finance.

Asness, C. S., Frazzini, A., Pedersen, L. H. (2012). *Leverage Aversion and Risk Parity.* Financial Analysts Journal, No. 1.

Bollerslev, T. (1986). *Generalized Autoregressive Conditional Heteroskedasticity.* Journal of Econometrics, No. 31.

Fama, E. F., French, K. R. (2004). *The Capital Asset Pricing Model: Theory and Evidence.* Journal of Economic Perspectives, 18(3).

Kelly Price, Barbara Price, Timothy J. Nantell (1982). *Variance and Lower Partial Moment Measures of Systematic Risk: Some Analytical and Empirical Results*. Journal of Finance, No. 3.

Kenton, W. (2024). *What Beta Means for Investors*. Investopedia.

Linciano, N., Soccorso, P. (2012). *La rilevazione della tolleranza al rischio degli investitori attraverso il questionario*. CONSOB, July.

Markowitz, H. (1952). *Portfolio Selection*. Journal of Finance, 7.

Pratt, J. W. (1964). *Risk Aversion in the Small and in the Large*. Econometrica, 32(1–2).

Sharpe, W. F. (1964). *Capital Asset Prices: A Theory of Market Equilibrium under Conditions of Risk*. Journal of Finance, 19(3).

Books

Bodie, Z., Kane, A., Marcus, A. J. (2020). *Investments*. McGraw-Hill Education.

Colombo, M. (2024). *Strategic Adjustment and Quantitative Risk Management*.

Dowd, K. (2002). *Measuring Market Risk*. Wiley.

Elton, E. J., Gruber, M. J., Brown, S. J., Goetzmann, W. N. (2014). *Modern Portfolio Theory and Investment Analysis*. Wiley.

Hull, J. C. (2015). *Risk Management and Financial Institutions*. Wiley.

Jorion, P. (2007). *Value at Risk: The New Benchmark for Managing Financial Risk*. McGraw-Hill.

J.P. Morgan/Reuters. (1996). *RiskMetrics – Technical Document*.

Luenberger, D. G. (1998). *Investment Science*. Oxford University Press.

Miller, M. B. (2019). *Quantitative Financial Risk Management*. Wiley.

Qian, E. (2011). *Risk Parity Portfolios: Efficient and Diversified*. PanAgora Asset Management.

Tsay, R. S. (2010). *Analysis of Financial Time Series* (3rd ed.). Wiley-Interscience.

Von Neumann, J., Morgenstern, O. (1944). *Theory of Games and Economic Behavior*. Princeton University Press.

ACKNOWLEDGMENTS

Writing this book has been a true personal journey. Every page, every concept, has represented for me not only an exploration into the field of finance, but also a moment of growth and self-understanding, of the discipline itself, and of the best way to communicate it clearly and meaningfully.

And finally, thank you, reader. If you have chosen to turn these pages, it means that my work has sparked a genuine interest. Your curiosity and the time you have devoted to this book make all of this profoundly meaningful. I sincerely hope that the analyses, ideas, and tools presented here will prove useful to you—both for gaining a deeper understanding of risk dynamics and for inspiring further reflections in your financial or professional activity.

Your small gesture makes a difference

If you have found value in this book, I would be truly grateful if you could take a moment to leave a review. Your words can help other readers discover this work and, above all, they represent genuine feedback and encouragement for me. Thank you from the bottom of my heart for your support and for sharing in this reading experience.

Thank you once again for your support.

Davide Colombo

www.ingramcontent.com/pod-product-compliance
Lightning Source LLC
LaVergne TN
LVHW022315200926
848481LV00004B/1353